"This book remiourselves. I just threw out

my coffee can with

the bacon grease in it—

and I miss it."

—Congresswoman
Maxine Waters

Sckraight from the Ghetto

You Know You're Ghetto If...

**Bertice Berry, Ph.D, and
Joan Coker, M.D.**

 St. Martin's Griffin ⚞ New York

Design by Gretchen Achilles

ISBN 0-312-15448-8

10 9

This book is dedicated to our mothers,
Beatrice and Beatrice, who taught us to
never forget where we came from.

Acknowledgments

I'd like to acknowledge all the ghetto contributors. Special thanks to Tia Thompson and family for their years of support and for scoring 450 on the Ghetto Test, and Ericka Majors, Will Downing, and Wally Collins for their unsolicited input. Victoria Sanders, our literary agent, the winner of the **white woman who gets it** award, three years in a row. Caledonia Kearns for being Victoria's voice of reason, and Diane for putting up with Victoria. The team at St. Martin's: Jennifer Weis, my editor; Madeleine Findley; Tara Watts; Glenda Howard; Catherine Spencer; and Jamie Brickhouse for realizing the truth of the big picture. Without all of you none of this would have been possible, **'CAUSE WE ALL GHETTO!**

—Dr. Bertice Berry

Acknowledgments (cont.)

For my mother, "Bebe" Ross Coker, and father, Lawrence Coker, Jr., for continued encouragement, love, and support in all that I do. My sisters, Laurie, Julie, and Ayesha for impeccable wit, love, laughter, and faith. To all of my family—thanx for wonderful memories. To Dr. Kim A. Brittingham and family, the crew from Wilmington, Delaware, and Tuskegee "Institute" University family—"Ya know ya ghetto"—and I love it! A very special thanx to the Department of Otolaryngology for allowing me this time, and for its continued support, and the entire King/Drew Medical Center family in Los Angeles. Victoria Sanders—thank you for creating this opportunity. Coauthor Dr. Bertice Berry—this was truly a blast from our past.

—Joan Coker, M.D.

Introduction

According to *Webster's Dictionary*, the word *ghetto* was originally defined as a section to which Jews were formerly restricted. Over time a ghetto was thought of as any section of a city in which members of some minority group live or to which they are restricted by discrimination. Later on, the word *ghetto* was reduced to a more narrow connotation. It commonly referred to an area populated by lower-class African Americans.

More recently, however, the word *ghetto* has taken on a whole new meaning. This meaning is much more inclusive, so much so that there is a great deal of confusion as to what ghetto is, and what ghetto ain't, who ghetto is or who ghetto ain't, who's more ghetto than whom, et cetera, et cetera, et cetera, ad nauseam, ad infinitum, Amen!

After a great deal of painstaking observation and research, we the authors/ghettologists, Joan Coker, M.D., and Bertice

Berry, Ph.D., have put together a collection of ghettoisms. Usually research conducted on subgroups is conducted by members outside that group. Not so with us. Coker is an otolaryngologist (We know it's a big word, but white people can't say it either. Just say *ENT*), and Berry is a sociologist/comedian. We ourselves are recovering ghetto-ites.

In *Sckraight from the Ghetto* we give an in-depth, up-close, up-way-too-close analysis of ghettoism. Not until now has anyone given the overlooked ghetto-ite a safe haven wherein it is possible to confess in a loud, very loud, extremely loud, talk-back-to-the-movie-screen-voice the following affirmation: "Hi my name is Sheliaquanda, and I'm ghetto." Then, and only then, can the healing begin.

This book will be a major contributor to the annals of human behavior. Obviously there is a demand for it. We are merely filling the void.

Webster Was Wrong

Ghetto is not where you live. It does not refer to an area comprised primarily of one racial or ethnic group. Ghetto is not about one's income or social status. *Ghetto is a state of mind. Mine and yours.*

When we first approached the publishing world with this book, the response was tremendous—tremendously negative. There was much concern on the part of those kind and well-meaning white folks, you know, the ones who are constantly reminding you that they have a black friend. Their concern was that this book might be racist. Which was a coincidence since *You Might Be a Racist* is the title of our upcoming book. It includes such wise proverbs as "You might be a racist if you think you can define racism better than the people who experience it."

We decided to test the book on the real public, you know, the folks who actually buy books. Early readings of

Sckraight from the Ghetto, to African American and other ghetto audiences, were overwhelmingly positive. The only problem we encountered was trying to get away from listeners who always seemed to have one more ghetto to add. These amateurs felt that they could top us, the noted ghettologists, at our own game. It was only when we pointed out how ghetto they were that they stopped trying to negotiate a deal for a cut of our book royalties.

We must admit that we were not prepared for the incredible response to these early readings of *Sckraight from the Ghetto.* Church groups, high-sidity folks, the young, the old, everybody and their mother identified. Proof that you can take a person out of the ghetto, but it's hard to get the ghetto from under one's acrylic nails, out of a six-foot weave, or off the car one drives all the way to the park to wax.

We were pleasantly surprised by the stimulating conversations that the ghettoisms evoked. For many they initiated a stroll down memory lane. A lane that was ofttimes riddled with pain, a lane that screams, "Yes, Langston, life has been a crystal stair." No matter what the image, *Sckraight from the Ghetto* reminds us of home.

The conversations and laughter always led to discussions on community improvement and personal healing. Even when the ghettoisms struck home, they did so with a positive outcome.

So now that you know how moved you will be, and how deep we are, let's get a few things clear about what ghetto is and what ghetto ain't.

A Few Ghetto Facts

➡ All African Americans are not ghetto, but they know someone who is. This person is commonly referred to as "my play cousin."

➡ Ghetto is a black thing but you too can understand. Ghetto cuts across the color barrier. There are Caucasian ghetto-ites. These individuals are commonly referred to as "Heidi, my play cousin."

- All poor people are not ghetto. Some wealthy people are, e.g., Whitney Houston, Bobby Brown (see item on Ghetto Weddings), LaToya and Michael Jackson (see item on baby hair), Jesse Jackson and Johnny Cochran (see item on rhyming in the workplace).

- Once ghetto is not always ghetto. There are reformed ghetto-ites. (This is not to be confused with a Reform Jew. Note: There is no "ed" on the end of the religious type.) E.g., *Eddie Murphy* (see item on red leather in the workplace), *Janet Jackson* (see item on "It's all relative, and yours are ghetto"), *We the authors* (you don't need to see no item we told you we ain't ghetto no more, ugh, we mean any longer).

Okay, enough about what the book is about. You've got it, so sit your ghetto self down, read, and let the healing begin.

p.s.

There is also a Ghetto Test. Don't try to avoid it or silently administer it to others. It was included for those of you who may still be in denial. It proves beyond the shadow of The Shadow whether or not you are ghetto. Enjoy.

YOu KnOW yOu're Ghetto If...

1. The only TV in your house that works is the ten-inch black-and-white and it's sitting on top of the inoperative floor model.

2. There's reusable bacon grease in a Maxwell House can in the center of the burners on your stove.

3. You own a crocheted tissue box or toilet paper cover with a doll's head on top.

4. Your pillowcase has more than five uses (e.g., laundry bag, luggage, dust rag, ice pack, infant blanket, towel, washcloth, placemat—you get the point).

5. You have a picture of the Black Trinity—Jesus, Martin Luther King, Jr., and John F. Kennedy.

6. Your lampshade still has the plastic on it.

All Up in My House

YOu KnOW yOu're Ghetto If...

7. Your bedspread had that lumpy floral pattern, and you picked the fuzzy balls out, and your mother beat you and said, "That's why we can't have nothing nice."

8. There is a kitchen chair with exposed padding on the front porch.

9. Your bed has slats.

2

10. Your screen window has no screen.

11. The exhaust fan over your stove works better when it's off.

12. You have a plastic runner in the living room that throws everyone one hundred feet when they attempt to walk on it. (Note: Tack that bad boy down.)

13. The only form of art in your house is the naked lady lamp that drips oil.

YOu KnOW yOu're Ghetto If...

14. You use a pair of pliers to change the channel on your TV.

15. You've never had anything professionally repaired. (Child, Uncle Booky will fix it.)

16. Turning up the heat means turning on another burner on the stove.

17. The batteries in your remote control are held in place with a piece of tape.

18. There is foil or a hanger on your TV antenna.

19. You have project heat. (Note: This means that you have to open your window in the winter.)

20. You use a can of Bon Ami to hold your bathroom window up.

21. All of your windows are painted shut.

All Up in My House

YOu KnOw yOu're Ghetto If...

22. Your baby's shoe doubles as a door stop.

23. You use the same light bulbs for four different lamps.

24. You have French Provencial furniture.

25. The Antebellum South is a theme for anything.

26. You leave your Christmas lights up all year.

4

27. All of the pot holders in your house were made at summer camp.

28. You have a bag of wrapping bows and boxes that came from presents you got years ago.

29. Something smells spoiled in the refrigerator, and all you do is change the box of Arm & Hammer baking soda.

30. Your drinking glasses used to be jelly jars.

All Up in My House

YOu KnOW yOu're Ghetto If...

31. Your old tire is now your planter.

32. Your furniture is covered in plastic.

33. You have unbreakable dishes and you don't have children.

34. You run to get pots as soon as it rains.

35. You have a brown stain on your ceiling.

5

36. The roaches in your house only come out when company comes.

37. Your telephone is still a rotary and has an extra-loud ringer.

38. Your lampshade has a stain and you turn it toward the wall.

39. You still refer to your stereo as the hi-fi.

All Up in My House

YOu KnOW yOu're Ghetto If...

40. You refer to your dresser as "the bureau."

41. You refer to the refrigerator as an icebox.

42. You think of paneling as a home improvement.

43. You have faux wood paneling wallpaper.

44. You decorate your home in the same style as the ones your great-grandmother had to clean.

45. You insulate your home with heavy plastic and tape.

46. You have a lamp that has no shade.

47. You have to unscrew the light bulb to turn your lamp off or on.

48. You've ever used a coat as a blanket.

49. The shag carpet in your home is now more like a flat-top.

YOu KnOW yOu're Ghetto If...

50. The back of your toilet seat is always off, and you know how to manually flush it.

51. Your glasses and silverware came from a gas station.

52. You have more dishes in your bedroom than in your kitchen.

53. You never clean the ring out of your tub, hoping that it will magically disappear.

8

54. You have ever raked, swept, or watered your dirt yard.

YOu KnOW YOu're Ghetto If...

55. You have more than ten uses for Vaseline, and one of them is shoe polish.

56. You don't think you're clean unless there is visible baby powder on your neck and chest, and you ain't even no baby.

57. You look greasy. (Note: We had lots of examples, but our goal is not to offend, nay to heal.)

58. The heels of your feet look like you've been kicking flour.

59. Your collar is still up.

60. You wear any of the following: Brute, Hai Karate, Jean Nâté, Old Spice, Chloe, English Leather, Charlie, Fabergé.

61. You use Tussy.

YOu KNOW yOu're Ghetto If...

62. You use black eye liner to line your lips.

63. Your lipstick matches your clothes.

64. You run out of the 3 for .99 plastic caps, and you use a plastic grocery bag to cover your head instead.

65. You have rolls in the back of your neck.

66. You wear your shower cap everywhere but in the shower.

67. You dry-clean your washable clothing (e.g., jeans, T-shirts, baseball jersey, etc.).

68. You wrap your teeth in tissue.

69. You run out of toothpaste and you use the box of baking soda that's been absorbing odors from the refrigerator.

70.
You've never been to the dentist.

YOu KNOW yOu're Ghetto If...

71. You clean your teeth with a matchbook or business card.

72. You clean your ears with a bobby pin, key, or ink pen cap.

73. You wear your clothes with a tag on them.

74. You don't remove the cloth label from the sleeve of your suit jacket.

75. You iron dirty clothes.

76. You have a keloid on your ear and you still wear earrings.

77. Your bathroom medicine cabinet is filled with Avon's Skin So Soft.

Ghetto Grooming

YOu KnOW yOu're Ghetto If...

78. You got in a fight with your brother, Brother, because he had a crease around his head, and you automatically knew he had stolen your pantyhose to make a stocking cap.

79. The only art you own is on your fingernails.

80. You've ever used a cold biscuit to polish your shoes.

13

YOu KnOW yOu're Ghetto If...

Ghetto Hair

81. Your husband's hair requires more rollers than yours.

82. Your comb has three teeth and you still use it.

83. Your weave is longer than your torso.

84. You still use any of the folllowing: Sulfur 8, Dixie Peach, Bergamont, Dax, Murray's, Tuxedo, Ultra Sheen.

85. You parted your hair in the center of your head and slapped grease across the front of it and referred to it as "my baby hair."

86. Your hair leaves a stain on the rear passenger window.

87. You still wear, or want to wear, bangs or a mushroom.

88. You go to a barber for a blow-out or shape-up.

YOu KnOW yOu're Ghetto If...

89. You go to a beauty salon for a press and curl.

90. You've ever waited several hours in a salon to get your hair done and you had an appointment.

91. Your daughter has a barrette on every extension.

92. Your daughter is under sixteen and has extensions.

93*. You've ever asked, "How my waves look?" (As in finger waves.)

15

94. Your daughter's ribbons are ten inches longer than her ponytail.

95. You have burns on your ears from the straightening comb or curling iron.

96*. You perm your five-year-old's hair.

YOu KnOW yOu're Ghetto If...

97. Your hair won't move and it's not short.

98. You decorate your hair with any of the following: glitter, rhinestones, glue, gold spray, or Kool-Aid. (Note: these items are for arts and crafts.)

99. You spend more time combing your hair than you do studying.

16

100. You have to put a towel on your furniture so that your curl activator won't stain it.

101. Your wig is bigger than the hat that's on it.

102. You refer to the hair at the nape of your neck as your "kitchen."

Ghetto Hair

103*. You ever got your hair did, fixed, fried, dyed, or laid to the side.

YOu KNOW yOu're Ghetto If...

104. You still think there's such a thing as "good" or "bad" hair. (Note: It's not the hair, it's the brain under it.)

105. Your roots are a different color from your hair.

106. Your baby has a bow or barrette on her one strand of hair.

107*. You're on a first-name basis with the Korean lady in the wig store.

108. You still part your hair down the middle. (Note: Old ghetto, or retro-ghetto, it's all the same.)

109. Due to excess pulling, your hairline starts at your ears.

110. You have those little white bumps around your head because your hair's too tight.

Ghetto Hair

YOu KnOW yOu're Ghetto If...

111. There's more hair on your bathroom floor and in your sink than there is on your head.

112. You never learned to swim because you couldn't get your hair wet.

Ghetto Hair

It's All in a Name

113. Your name is spelled phonetically.

114. Your nickname is the opposite of your appearance, e.g., Shorty, and you're six foot, five hundred pounds, or Redbone and you're blacker than Mickey's ears (the mouse, damn it.)

115*. Your child thinks his real name is Little Man.

116. You changed your first name 'cause you said it was the white man's, but you kept your last name—your real slave name.

117*. You have trouble spelling your children's names, and you named them.

118. You've changed the pronunciation of your name, but you keep the spelling the same (e.g., Rachel–Roshell, Sade–Shade, Jackie–Jackee. Okay, she actually changed the spelling, but you get the point.).

119. You had your unpronounceable name designed in a piece of jewelry.

120. You were named after any of the Jacksons or any character from *Roots*.

121. You're known by the positioning of your feet and legs (i.e., pigeon-toed, slew-footed, bow-legged, knock-kneed).

YOu KnOw yOu're Ghetto If...

122. You have actually invited someone to talk to your hand.

123. You weigh more than three hundred pounds, but you claim that you can't eat everybody else's food.

124. You threaten anyone who comes near the corn on your baby toe or the bunion on your big toe.

125. Every fashion show you've attended was also a hair, craft, or variety show.

126. You have razor bumps on the back of your neck.

127. You've ever dropped anything and kissed it up to God.

128. Your TV and stereo are always on at the same time.

The Things We Do

YOu KnOW yOu're Ghetto If...

129. You still eat at Denny's.

130*. You've ever called a radio station for anything.

131. You've ever screamed on a radio station before you even heard what your prize was.

132. You think that every line in a movie theater requires your loud response.

24

133. When you're discriminated against at a store you buy tons of stuff to prove to the clerks that you can.

134. You've ever parked your car in the middle of the street for hours.

135. You're over eighteen and you've never voted in a presidential election, but you're constantly complaining about the state of the union.

136.
You
page
yourself.

YOu KnOW yOu're Ghetto If...

137.   You own a tip card, and you use it.

138.   You're late for everything, and you try to act like it's a cultural expression.

139.   You use the bathroom with the door open.

140*.   You come out of the bathroom and ask for a pack of matches instead of air freshener.

26

141.   You light your cigarette on a stove.

142.   **You're afraid of your own people.**

143.   You call people long-distance to talk about the soap operas.

144.   You call people locally to talk about the soaps.

145.   You talk about the soaps.

The Things We Do

YOu KnOW yOu're Ghetto If...

146. You set your watch fifteen or thirty minutes fast and you're still always late.

147. You show up to events because you know that there will be freebies.

148. You get drunk and brag about it.

149. You think that you can smell rain.

150. You put an empty ice tray in the freezer.

151. You put a large container that has only one drop of whatever it had left in it back in the refrigerator.

152. People can hear you breathing and you ain't even asleep.

153. After twenty years of using a headset you finally figure out that there is a left and right earphone.

27

The Things We Do

154. Your key ring has so many keys on it that people think you're a janitor.

YOu KNOW yOu're Ghetto If...

155. You keep a coat hanger in your purse because you know you're going to lock your keys in your car.

156. You have so much food on your face that other people can feel it, but still you don't.

157*. No one is allowed in your home after New Year's until a man has come through the door.

158. You give directions vis-a-vis fast food restaurants.

29

159. You follow the fire truck or any other emergency vehicle.

160. You shop at a store that's lined with Plexiglas.

161. You shop where you can buy one item and get three free.

It's All Relative and Yours Are Ghetto

162. None of your aunts or uncles is in any way related to your mother or father.

163. You have a brother named Brother.

164. You had to take your little brother or sister everywhere you went.

165*. You refer to your boyfriend as "My Baby Daddy."

166. There is a wall, table, or curio full of pictures of every relative known to you, but even more of those who aren't.

167. Everybody in your family talks at the same time.

168. You can't watch TV without seeing someone who looks exactly like somebody you know.

169. Your mother cleaned floors to educate you, and now you think that you're better than her.

yOu KnOw yOu're Ghetto If...

170. You have an uncle who is both a drunk and a genius.

171. Your drunk uncle comes in, and your whole family says, "Oh Lord."

172*. Your family members are related to you on both sides.

32

173. You have a brother named Stink, Booh, or Pookie.

174. You're working on a graduate degree and your family keeps saying, "I thought you already graduated."

175. The only time your family gets together is when somebody dies.

176. You can't remember your mother's address, but you can still sing the address to Zoom.

It's All Relative and Yours Are Ghetto

YOu KnOW yOu're Ghetto If...

177. You ever ordered anything from a Flagbrothers catalog.

178. You carry a purse with a jogging suit.

179. There's a nail coming out of your pumps, and you still wear them.

180*. You look like a walking advertisement for a sportswear company and you don't have an endorsement contract.

181. Your shoes are run over in two directions and everyone can tell but you.

182. You wear white stockings and you're not a nurse.

183*. You have hundreds of college sweatshirts but you claim you can't afford to go to college.

YOu KNOW yOu're Ghetto If...

184. You have ever worn any of the following:

➡ A gold chain with a Mercedes symbol

➡ Gazelle frames

➡ A Kangol

➡ Tailor Mades (the pants)

➡ Multiple zippers on jacket or pants

➡ Sun visors in the nineties (see O.J. Simpson)

➡ Stirrups, pumps, and socks—all at once

➡ Cowboy boots with a skirt

➡ A do-rag

➡ Stocking cap

➡ A silk black vest with anything

➡ A vest with glitter—correction, any clothes with glitter

Bad Rags/Ghetto Clothes

YOu KnOW yOu're Ghetto If...

➡ Colored stockings, baby-doll socks, and pumps

➡ Leg warmers and a skirt

➡ A sweater tied around your neck—and you've never played tennis

185. You wear your Easter outfit to school the Monday after Easter.

186. You still get Easter outfits.

35

187. You feel compelled to wear a belly shirt, exposing your many rolls of fat, and you think you look "da bomb."

188. Every pair of underwear you own has a little hole in them—from merely picking.

189. You've ever sewn a crease in your jeans.

190. You've ever used bleach to write your initials in your jeans

YOu KnOW yOu're Ghetto If...

191. You don't feel quite right about being at an amusement park unless you're dressed exactly like at least one other person.

192. You have an uncle who wears leisure suits.

193. Your clothes look like you had to jump off a roof to get into them.

194. You dry your clothes with an iron.

37

195. You've ever worn wet underwear.

Bad Rags/Ghetto Clothes

YOu KnOW yOu're Ghetto If...

196. You keep all of your prized possessions in a Crown Royal bag.

197. You wear flip-flops outside the house.

198. You wear dance shoes and you're not on stage.

199. You're a man and you think that it's your God-given right to wear your hat inside, or anywhere else you please.

200. You have any symbols, designs, or letters cut into your hair. (Dennis Rodman, this includes you.)

201*. You're known for rolling any of the following: your neck, your eyes, your *r*'s, or your wrist.

yOu KnOw yOu're Ghetto If...

202.   You stop your car in the middle of the street to talk to one of your play cousins.

203*.   You're good at playing numbers but not adding them.

204.   You prefer the back of the bus.

Ghetto Linguistics

205. You answer the phone and add the letter *m* before your greeting (i.e., mmm–yello).

206. You've ever said:

→ "Whatever."

→ "Forget chu din, forget you, forgot you, I never thought about chu."

→ "Shut up. Shut don't go up, prices do. Ask your mamma and she'll tell you too."

→ "You play too much."

→ "I took and told."

→ "I don't *even* know."

→ "Psyche."

→ "Why you tripping?"

What Chu Talkin' 'Bout

YOu KnOw yOu're Ghetto If...

➜ "Ooh, yoke."

➜ "Stop riding off of me."

➜ "Snap."

➜ "Kiss what I twist and I don't mean my wrist."

207*. Your mouth makes the shape of the word before you say it.

208. You laugh your head off before you tell a joke that ain't even funny.

209. You answer any question by beginning your response with the following phrase: "The reason being is . . ."

210. Your bottom-line phrase always begins with the following: "My whole thing is this . . ."

What Chu Talkin' 'Bout

211. You're constantly referring to everything as "Wack."

YOu KnOW yOu're Ghetto If...

212. You complete each sentence with the following phrase: "Know what I'm saying?"

213. You've ever referred to the wind as the Hawk.

214*. You add "ed" or "t" to the end of a word that's already in the past tense (e.g., tooked, light-skinneded, kilt, ruint).

215. You say "Yet and still."

216. Whistling takes the place of an exclamation point.

217. You refer to more than one person as "G."

218. You speak CB lingo even when you're not on one (e.g., That's a big 10–4, Mom).

219. You answered "President" when the roll was called.

What Chu Talkin' 'Bout

YOu KnOw YOu're Ghetto If...

220. The person you're speaking to doesn't speak any English and you just talk louder.

221. You talk loud on the phone because it's long distance.

222. You have to walk around the room to laugh.

223. You ever referred to your house as a crib, your job as a gig or slave, or money as bread.

44

224*. You refer to getting drunk as any of the following: messed up, sauced, toasted, tore-up-from-the-floor-up, nice, pickled, ripped, buzzed.

225*. You refer to making love as any of the following: knocking the boots, trim, break me off a piece, somping, somping (something, something), poontang, gettin' some, snatch, doin' it, pussy, bootie call, gettin' your groove on.

YOu KnOW yOu're Ghetto If...

226*. You use any of the following words to describe bodily eliminations: poop, dookey, piss, take a leak, take a dump, go to see a man about a dog . . . you get the point.

227. You've ever referred to anything as one of the following: do-hickey, thing-a-ma-bob, whoseywhats, whatchamacallit.

You use but mispronounce these words:

Ghetteloquilisms

228. Ambalamps—Ambulance

229. Skrimps or Strimps—Shrimp
(Note: there is no *s* on the end.)

230. Pacific vs. Specific (Note: These are not interchangeable. In order to determine which is appropriate, listen to clues such as references to large bodies of water, as opposed to that body of water.)

231. Skreet—Street

232. Axe—ask

233. Look Dead—Looked

234. Member—Of or pertaining to a recollection (e.g., ya'll member the time . . .?)

YOu KnOw yOu're Ghetto If...

You use but mispronounce these words:

235. Spisketti–Spaghetti

236. Zinc–Sink

237. Alblums–What we used before CDs

238. Showliz–That sure is

239. Wayment–Wait a minute

240. Nem–contraction for *and them* (e.g., I can't wait 'til Clevon nem get here.)

47

YOu KnOW yOu're Ghetto If...

241. You got your ears pierced with a needle that your play cousin heated up on a stove and you kept the hole open with a "sterilized" broomstraw or thread for approximately 21–30 days.

242. You held your knee socks up with rubber bands.

243. You wear socks as a glove and you're not an infant.

244. You wear suspenders and a belt at the same time.

245*. You've ever polished your sneakers.

246. You have two different pairs of pantyhose, and both have a run in them, so you cut off the damaged legs and then wear both at the same time. ('Gone with your bad self.)

YOu KnOw yOu're Ghetto If...

247.   You put fingernail polish on pantyhose to keep a run from getting worse.

248.   Your stockings come packaged in an egg.

249.   You buy your stockings at the same place you do your grocery shopping.

250.   You put metal taps on the bottoms of your shoes, and you don't tap.

251.   You wanted to walk in heels so badly that you crushed the centers of soda cans with your foot and walked around in them like they were new shoes.

252.   The doilies on your furniture double as a head cover for prayer service.

253.   You have a pair of house slippers to match all of your short sets.

254. The best pair of shoes you own are sneakers.

YOu KnOw yOu're Ghetto If...

255. You folded your socks over to cover a hole, but now your shoes don't fit because of the lump in them.

256. You purposely bought your child's shoes two sizes too large.

257. You tell all of your business because your shoes are too small. (Yes, there is a connection.)

258*. You wear colored contacts. PERIOD.

51

259. You have multiple holes in your ears, but none of your earrings matches.

260. Your indoor skates had a gazillion pom-poms on them.

261. You wear a short set with church socks and shoes.

262. You lose your earring back and you replace it with the eraser of a number-two pencil.

263. You wear a watch that you know doesn't work.

264. You can't buy a pair of shoes without dancing in them first.

265. You have more shoes than you have books.

52

YOu KnOW yOu're Ghetto If...
(Gettin' Your Grub On)

266. There is a Maxwell House coffee can full of recycled bacon grease in the center of the burners on your stove.

267. You drink wine regularly, but have never needed a corkscrew.

268*. You think of Kool-Aid as a member of one of the major food groups.

269*. You think of fatback as a source of nutrition. (Note: There is no such thing as low-fat fatback.)

270. You put catsup on your eggs or any other breakfast food.

271. You use salt before you taste your food.

So Good It'll Make You Wanna Smack Your Mamma

YOu KNOW YOu're Ghetto If...

272. You use catsup on anything other than a hot dog, french fries, or hamburger.

273. You suck the marrow out of a chicken bone—in a restaurant.

274. Your kitchen canisters are filled with something other than what they're labeled for (e.g., coupons, rice, beans, important papers, and bacon grease).

54

275*. You eat a chicken sandwich with the bone still in it.

276. You put a used tea bag in the refrigerator.

277. The only choice of breakfast cereals you had was Puffa Puffa Wheat or Puffa Puffa Rice.

278. You save food from the airplane so you can eat it at home.

279*.
You're constantly chewing, and there's nothing in your mouth.

YOu KnOW yOu're Ghetto If...

280. You feel a need to make noise when you eat, and then you have the nerve to inform those around you that in Japan this noise is considered a compliment to the cook. (Note: You are not in Japan nor are you Japanese.)

281. You got angry when the government stopped the cheese program.

282*. Every time you have macaroni and cheese, you feel a need to comment on how nothing makes it better than "the gobment cheese."

56

283. You know how to melt government cheese.

284. You can remember canning thousands of jars of fruits, preserves, and jellies, but you don't know what happened to them.

285. You go into a McDonald's drive-through with five different orders and you're constantly changing them.

YOu KnOw yOu're Ghetto If...

286. You're always eating at other people's houses, but you never bring anything.

287. After you've eaten tons of food at someone else's house you have the audacity to ask for a piece of foil so you can take some home.

288. You eat syrup sandwiches.

289. You prefer the meatless neck bone to a hearty chicken breast.

57

290. You put gravy on everything, especially biscuits.

291. You claim to be a vegetarian but you eat meat on weekends.

292. You ever thought that coffee would make you black.

So Good It'll Make You Wanna Smack Your Mamma

293. You put your salted peanuts in the bottom of your Coca-Cola.

YOu KnOW yOu're Ghetto If...

294. You drink Slim·Fast or any other diet beverage along with your regular meal.

295. Someone says, "Smells like something is burning," and you're not fazed because you know that it's just the old food that's been in the bottom of your oven for weeks.

296. You eat cough drops like they're candy.

297. Blood comes out of your "cooked" chicken and you eat it anyway.

59

298. You put wet bread in your meat loaf.

299. You think catsup and spaghetti sauce are interchangeable.

300. You use neck bones or salt pork for seasoning.

301. You eat oatmeal because it sticks to your ribs on a cold day.

YOu KnOw yOu're Ghetto If...

302. You pop or crack your gum.

303. You ever ate fried bologna sandwiches, and liked them.

304. You put ice in your wine or beer.

305. Your idea of a fine wine is Boone's Farm or Ripple.

60

306. The only Chinese food that you'll eat is shrimp fried rice.

307*. Every time someone suggests Chinese food, you comment on how all the dogs in the neighborhood are disappearing.

308. You use bread to sop up your gravy.

309. You're at church and people can tell what you'll be having for dinner from the smell of your coat.

So Good It'll Make You Wanna Smack Your Mamma

yOu KnOw yOu're Ghetto If...

310. You cook chitterlings in a pressure cooker, and you put white bread on top to soak up the smell.

311*. You eat chitterlings with spaghetti.

312*. You eat chitterlings, period.

313. You've eaten so much Spam that you've figured out the ingredients.

314. You eat these ghetto snacks: pork rinds, chitterlings, Moon Pies with coke, pistachios, sunflower seeds, pumpkin seeds, licorice, salt and vinegar chips, Now and Laters (especially grape), those little juice-filled wax candies, Pixie Stix, Twisters, Bom Pops, Push-ups, Mary Janes, Lemon Heads, Boston Baked Beans, Mr. Softee, Redhots, Freezpops, Chick o Stix, Snowballs, Jiffy Pop, Cheez Whiz, Pop-Tarts, that candy that was stuck to paper—you know, those multicolored dots—Blowpops, candy necklaces, jawbreakers, the Sugar family—Sugar Daddy, Sugar Mama, Sugarbabies.

YOu KnOW yOu're Ghetto If...

315. You drink these ghetto beverages: Yoo-Hoo, Malt Liquor, Tahitian Treat, Sugar Water, Fanta Orange, Red Kool-Aid (even after Jim Jones), Red Dog, anything red, anything that costs .99 and comes in a gallon jug, Tab, Fresca, Water Ice, Hawaiian Punch, strawberry soda, pineapple soda, cream soda.

So Good It'll Make You Wanna Smack Your Mamma

YOu KnOW yOu're Ghetto If...

316. The rear window of your car is filled with stuffed animals.

317. You have a neon light around your license plate, rear brake light, or under your car.

318. The rear light of your car is broken and your idea of replacing it is taping it up and painting it red.

319. One of your car doors is a different color from the rest of the car.

320. You have a crack across your front windshield and you never bother to get it fixed.

321. You have more than one of the pine-scented Christmas tree air fresheners hanging from your rearview mirror.

Check Out My Ride

YOu KnOw yOu're Ghetto If...

322*. Your car cost more than your house.

323. The speakers in your Pinto belong in a nightclub.

324. Your rims on your car cost more than your car.

325. Your cellular phone cost more than your car.

326. Your car is cleaner than you are.

327. Your car is fifteen years old but has the "new car" scented air freshener.

328. You keep visible wax on your car from sunrise to sunset.

329*. You drive your car all the way to the park to wax it.

330. The leftover carpet from your house is on your dashboard.

Check Out My Ride

331. The outside of your car has fake wood on it.

You Know You're Ghetto If...

332. When asked, "What are your hobbies," you list your car.

333. You have bubbled or peeling tinted windows.

334. The trunk of your car is held closed with kite string, and no one in your family owns a kite.

335. There is anything on your antenna, including ribbons, balls, tiger tails, and tattered flags.

336. The only way to start the engine of the car is from under the hood.

337. You need a jump several times a day, and you don't own jumper cables.

338*. You own a Beamer or a Benz and you gas it up with $3.00 in coins.

Check Out My Ride

YOu KnOW yOu're Ghetto If...

339. You have so many parking tickets that you have to hide your car.

340. You drive around on the donut, months after the flat happened.

341. You prefer the visible white-wall tire.

342. You decorate your car like a Christmas tree.

343. Your car is pastel with a kit (detailwork).

344. You've ever used Coca-Cola to clean the rust off your car battery, and then drunk what's left.

345. Any of the following is your favorite car: BMW, Caddy, Gremlin, Hornet, Jeep Cherokee, Lincoln, Maxima, Nissan, Pacer, Pinto.

67

YOu KNOW yOu're Ghetto If...

346. You ask for change from the offering plate.

347. You put a sealed empty envelope in the church offering plate.

348*. Your pastor's car is longer than the church.

349. Your pastor's preaching sounds more like an asthma attack.

350. Your choir sings an "A" and "B" selection.

351. You can learn the latest dances from your church choir.

352*. The offering plate at your church goes around five times.

353. The announce-ments at your church are longer than the sermon.

354. Your child learned to divide by listening to the preacher take up an offering (e.g., We need $50.00. If I could get 50 people to give one dollar, 25 people to give $2, or 10 of God's anointed to give $5, et cetera, et cetera, et cetera . . .).

355. You can actually understand the devotional prayers of church members over sixty.

70

356. You think that you have your very own assigned seat in church and you lose your religion if anybody else sits in it.

357. You find yourself in competition with the pastor's wife for who's got on the biggest hat.

358. You leave the church before benediction so that you can be the first in line for the church dinner.

YOu KnOW yOu're Ghetto If...

359. You've ever used testimony time to tell somebody off.

360. You raise your right index finger every time you leave the church sanctuary. (Note: This is how our enslaved ancestors had to ask for permission to leave.)

Ghetto Church

YOu KNOW yOu're Ghetto If...

Ghetto Weddings

361. Either the bride or groom sings a solo to each other, or both.

362*. Nobody in the wedding can really fit in her dress, including the bride.

363. The reception is served buffet-style and on plastic-ware.

364. There is a DJ instead of a band.

365*. The reception meal was cooked by the bride's mother.

366. There's a raffle for the centerpieces at the end of the night.

367. The ceremony starts two hours late and nobody seems fazed.

368. It seems more like a concert.

YOu KnOW yOu're Ghetto If...

369. A fight breaks out.

370. There are more guests at the reception than there were at the wedding.

371. There are more people in the wedding than there are in the audience.

372. Everybody's exes were invited, because they're all remarried to somebody else in the family.

373*. Your wedding dress is also a maternity dress.

374*. The wedding march is actually a march.

375. You were the only black person at your wedding.

376. You sing ghetto wedding songs: "Always and Forever," "I'll Always Love You," "You and I," "Wind Beneath My Wings," "Here and Now," "Ribbon in the Sky," "For Always."

Ghetto Weddings

YOu KnOW yOu're Ghetto If...

377. The deceased and his widow are wearing matching outfits.

378. Someone tries to climb in the coffin.

379. The preacher is wearing shades.

380. A fight breaks out.

381*. More than one person thinks that he is the current spouse of the deceased.

382. The majority of the flowers at the burial site are plastic, and/or taken back the following day.

383. The service lasts for half a day.

384. Polaroid shots are being taken of the deceased.

Ghetto Funerals

YOu KNOW yOu're Ghetto If...

385*. No one knew the deceased by his real name. ("Who's Ravon Williams III, I thought his name was Bookie.")

386. Most of the mourners comment that the deceased didn't look that good when he was alive.

387. Everyone thought that the deceased looked like he was asleep.

76

388. You ever said that the deceased has "slipped away."

Ghetto Funerals

YOu KnOW yOu're Ghetto If...

389. You go out to a nightclub, but you stay outside in front of the club.

390. When you leave a club, you stand in front of someone else's nice car, hoping that folks will think that it's yours.

391. You and your friends get your picture taken in front of the wicker fan chair.

392*. You ever took a bus to a nightclub.

393. You go out dancing and you take that big old purse that you have to put on the floor in front of you.

394. You ask perfect strangers to take a picture with you, then you tell all of your friends that this is someone you actually dated.

YOu KnOw yOu're Ghetto If...

395. You get upset because the DJ didn't play the long version of the Electric Slide song.

396. The only song of the night that you dance to is the Electric Slide.

397. You go to a black club to pick up white women.

398. Your favorite nightclub has a secret knock.

78

399. You go to a club and ask for a setup.

400. There's a dress code but everyone looks like a reject from "American Bandstand."

YOu KnOW yOu're Ghetto If...

You hear or say any of the following phrases:

401. What's your sign?

402. Right about now we're gonna take a pause for the cause.

403. Let me introduce my band members, on my left, your right, is Smooth on the sax. On my right, your left, we got Bookie on keyboard...

404. Give the drummer some.

405. Right about now we gonna slow it down just a taste.

406. We need all the ladies for the Miss Lace, Big Booty, Big Legs, or Tootsie Roll contest.

407. Is you married?

YOu KnOw yOu're Ghetto If...

You hear or say any of the following phrases:

408. The color for tonight is black, and if you're wearing black you're all that.

409. Can I get those 7 digits?

410. Is ya'll twins? (reference to the fact that grown women who are not related, let alone twins, are dressing alike).

80

411. It's two of us and two of ya'll. What ya'll want to do?

412. Ya'll going to Denny's after this?

413. Da roof da roof da roof is on fire——————

414. Party over here, party right there, oooh, oooh. (Note: The oohs are done in a pitch high enough for a dog to hear.)

Ghetto Clubbing

YOu KnoW yOu're Ghetto If...

415*. You know all the words to "Float On."

416. Your favorite song has talking in it.

417. It takes you twenty minutes to sing a two-minute song.

418. You have all of Kenny G.'s CDs, but none of Gerald Albright's.

419. You only know the first line to "A House Is Not a Home," but you sing it anyway—in public.

420. You got into a fight with your cousin, Cuz, because he said that all of Lionel Richie's songs sound alike, but you think he's a musical genius.

421. You've been to more than one play with the word *Mamma* in the title.

422. You've won a Grammy for your B— and Ho rap record, and you start your acceptance speech with the following phrase: "First of all, I want to thank God, who is the head of my life."

YOu KnOW yOu're Ghetto If...

423. Any of the following is your favorite group:

➡ Climax

➡ The Brothers Johnson

➡ The Silvers

➡ Jodeci

➡ Ready for the World

➡ Tina Marie

➡ Tarvaris

➡ Commodores

➡ Fifth Dimension

➡ Jacksons/not the Jackson 5

➡ Osmonds (Psych)

Ghetto Music

God Bless the Child Whose Parents Are Ghetto

424. Your children's only form of entertainment is singing in the window fan.

425. Your child drops his pacifier, and you sanitize it by sucking on it.

426. You chew your baby's food and then feed it to them. (You ain't no bird. Stop acting like one.)

427. You're the teacher of an etiquette class and you call your students niggers.

428. You have to go through all your children's names before you can get to the one you want.

429*. You ever sent your children to pick out their own switch.

430.
You've ever been beaten with an extension cord.

YOu KNOW YOu're Ghetto If...

431. Your mother sounded like a rap artist when she was beating you.

432*. Your son is not even five years old, but he has his ears pierced.

433. **Your children don't know the words to "Punchinella" or "Miss Mary Mack," but they know the lyrics to all of Snoop Doggy Dogg's records.**

86

434. Your children go to school smelling like hot bacon grease.

435. **You pay more for your child's sneakers than you do for their childcare.**

436. You pinch your newborn's nose to make it thin.

God Bless the Child Whose Parents Are Ghetto

YOu KnOW YOu're Ghetto If...

437. Every child in the family has a different last name. (Note: This is not a criticism of single mothers. It is, however, a criticism of the fact that she doesn't think her name is better than that of the father who has nothing to do with his own child.)

438. You use abortion as a form of birth control.

God Bless the Child Whose Parents Are Ghetto

YOu KnOW yOu're Ghetto If...

439.   Your bike is missing one pedal.

440.   You ever played dodge ball.

441.   You ever played dodge ball with a ball that had no air in it.

442.   You ever played relivio. (By the way, what does relivio mean—is it Spanish for "to release"?)

443*.   You ever ran a race barefoot in the middle of the street at approximately eleven at night.

444.   You ever played kick the can.

445.   You ever played knuckles.

446.   Your name and/or astrological sign are inscribed on your basketball.

447.
Losing the ball meant that the game was over.

YOu KNOW yOu're Ghetto If...

448*. While you were playing basketball in the hot sun, your sneakers fell apart due to overbleaching.

449. Your basketball hoop has a rim but no net.

450. You thought that you were a gymnast because you could do a high flip on a pissy mattress that somebody threw out.

451. Walking across the room makes you sweat.

452. Your basketball hoop was made out of a milk carton.

453. You have a steering wheel instead of handlebars on your bike.

454. You've ever played Red-Light-Green-Light.

455. You've ever cheated in a game of Mother May I.

Ghetto Games

YOu KnOW yOu're Ghetto If...

456. You ride sideways on the bar of your play cousin's bike.

457. As a child your favorite pastime was dragging a stick along a metal fence so that you could hear the sound it made.

458. Going swimming meant turning on the fire hydrant.

91

YOu KnOW yOu're Ghetto If...

459. You kept the money from the candy sale fundraiser.

460. You pay one price and try to sneak into three different movies.

461. You sneak entire meals into the movies.

462*. Each time you go out with friends to eat, you ask "Who got me?" ("Who's paying for my portion?")

463. Your phone gets cut off every month despite the fact that you done told them people that the check is in the mail.

464. You write a check and you know that you don't have any money in the bank.

YOu KnOW yOu're Ghetto If...

465. You write a check to someone and you tell them to cash it quickly.

466*. You try to use someone else's nontransferable ticket to do anything, and then become irate when you can't.

467. You're constantly taking sick days off when you're not even sick and then you get mad when no one believes that you are.

468. Your phone bill has been in every child's name in your family.

469. Your three-year-old has bad credit.

470. You're constantly switching long-distance services so that you can get the freebies.

471. You've ever told the bill collector, "My mother said she ain't home."

YOu KnOW yOu're Ghetto If...

472. You've ever stolen from the paperboy.

473. You've ever sold or bought Amway.

YOu KnOw yOu're Ghetto If...

474. You ever thought of any of the following as a major factor in one's beauty: being double-jointed, bow-legged, having a gap between your teeth, having a mole, having light skin and long hair, having hairy legs.

475. You thought somone was fine because she had light eyes but only had three teeth.

476. You date white women, but you'll only marry a black one.

477. You date black women, but you'll only marry a white one.

YOu KnOW yOu're Ghetto If...

478. Your gold tooth is in the same place as your boyfriend's and they hit when you kiss and you think it's a sign.

479. You think your date is really the one because he took you to Red Lobster.

480*. You meet someone you like and you give them your beeper number, 'cause you live with somebody else.

481. You marry your prisoner pen pal who's on Death Row.

482. You write or scratch your loved one's name into anything that doesn't belong to you.

483. You think he's the one because he has a job.

484. You think he loves you because he only beat you once.

485. You think he's the one because he has a nice car.

Holidays

486. You decorate for every holiday.

487*. You think that Mother's Day comes on the first of every month.

YOu KnOW yOu're Ghetto If...

488. You put your gum behind your ear.

489*. You wait until you're in traffic to pick your nose.

490. You keep a reusable toothpick in your hair, mouth, or behind your ear.

491. You hang your pissy bed linen outside to air out, but never bother to wash it.

492. You know that your feet always stink, but you kick your shoes off anyway.

493. Your bedroom smells like you've been cooking socks.

494*. You eat boiled peanuts.

495. The earpiece on your phone is dirty.

Just Nasty

496*. You lick your fin-gers before you turn a page or count your money.

YOu KnOW yOu're Ghetto If...

497. You ate dirt because you heard that you have to eat dirt before you die.

498. You're finally able to suck that piece of food from between your teeth—and then you eat it.

499*. You prefer June Bug's grocery store because he's the only one who stocks hog maws, chitterlings, pickled pig feet, and headcheese.

101

500. There's more food in your drink than there was on your plate.

YOu KnOw yOu're Ghetto If...

Ghetto Pets

501*. You have no idea what the breed of your dog is.

502. Your dog has never had dog food (he just eats y'all's scraps).

503. You've ever buried any of your pets in the front yard.

504. Your dog's leash is a rope.

505*. Your dog's name is Rashid.

506. Your dog's name is Spanish and you aren't.

You Know You're Ghetto If...

507. The McDonald's in your neighborhood still sells strawberry sodas.

508. You thought that your neighborhood had its own call (you know, for safety purposes), then you discovered that every other neighborhood had the same call.

509. You have a Church's Chicken in your neighborhood.

510. Your neighborhood has more liquor stores than book stores.

511. All the businesses in your neighborhood are owned by people who don't live there.

512. Every week there's a new billboard advertising liquor, and you don't do anything about it.

YOu KnOW yOu're Ghetto If...

513. There is a crack house on your street and you and your neighbors try to ignore it.

514. You brag about being the only black in your neighborhood.

515. You litter your own neighborhood.

516. You tie your old pair of hightop Converses together, and throw them up over the outside telephone wire.

Ghetto Hood

YOu KnOW yOu're Ghetto If...

517. You go on a ten-hour trip and stop for nothing because you brought everything (e.g., chicken, deviled eggs, pickles, Funyuns, and those 10 for $1.00 sodas, especially black cherry).

518. The only vacation you've ever taken was to see your grandmother "Down South."

519. You've never missed a week of Def Comedy Jam, but you don't know who Moms Mabley is.

YOu KnOw yOu're Ghetto If...

You use these to cure everything:

Ghetto Cure-Alls

➡ Vicks VapoRub on your chest, under your nose, and down your throat

➡ Fletcher's Castoria

➡ Calamine lotion

➡ Cocoa butter

➡ Gargling with warm salt water

➡ *Butter on a burn (Note: This is good for popcorn but will not heal.)

➡ *Warm flat ginger ale (also known as ging-ale)

➡ Baby aspirin

➡ Cold compress

➡ Hot-water bottle

➡ Aloe vera plant

yOu knOw yOu're Ghetto If...

You use these to cure everything:

➡ Mercurochrome/iodine (you know, that red stuff)

➡ Peroxide

➡ Alcohol

➡ Baby oil

➡ AD Ointment

➡ Noxema

➡ Baking soda and vinegar

YOu KnOW yOu're Ghetto If...

This is a test. It is only a test. While much research and observation have gone into this work, we implore you, do not take yourself or the results of this test too seriously.

About the Test

Some items carry a heavier weight than others. These items are marked as follows: *.

Scoring

Scoring the ghetto test is a simple procedure and can be done rather painlessly. The pain comes with the realization of how ghetto one actually is.

Realization is necessary, however, in order to allow the healing process to begin. For every item that you answer yes to, give yourself one point, and add away.

YOu KnOw yOu're Ghetto If...

EXEMPT—This does not mean that you did well.

You are exempt from the Ghetto Test if you:

A. Skipped over the intro.

B. Read the book out of order.

C. Answered yes to any of the items marked *.

D. If you answered yes to either the first or second item in any category, then you are in a ghetto home, or have a ghetto car, or go to ghetto clubs, etc.

If you are exempt from the ghetto test it means that you are beyond the shadow of a doubt **GHETTO.**

YOu KnOW yOu're Ghetto If...

If You Scored:

5–10 items only: You are probably not ghetto. But you probably don't get out much either. We recommend that you call your mother, and father, or any other family member who is still in touch with the rest of your people.

10–49 items: You didn't add properly. Go back and add all items that apply to you and yours.

50–99 items: You were very careful as to how you answered, but whom do you think you're fooling? Retake the test, and this time tell the truth.

100–149 items: Yes, you're ghetto. But you've been away from your old stomping grounds.

150–259: Ghetto and in denial.

260 or more: You are ghetto. You are so ghetto that everyone associated with you is also ghetto. You are not alone.

We All Ghetto.

Ghetto Test

YOu KnOw yOu're Ghetto If...

Items Printed in Bold Letters

If you answered yes to any of the items in bold letters, *you are not ghetto.* As a matter of fact, you are anti-ghetto, and anti-self.

We recommend the following:

→ Pray, pray hard, pray very hard.

→ Get in touch with the truth about yourself and your people.

→ Find out who your people are, and see if they'll take you back.

→ Surround yourself with positive people. (Note: These are people who scored differently from you.)

→ Read Carter G. Woodson's *The Miseducation of the Negro.*

→ Ask yourself on a daily basis, "Why am I here?" Look for an answer.

111

YOu KnOW yOu're Ghetto If...

➡ Accept yourself and the beauty of your people.

➡ After begining the above steps retake the test and check for progress.